Dedication

To my brothers, Ritch, Ken, Matt and David

Edited by Sandy Livoti
Cover design by Travis Bryant
Interior design by Lora Westberg

All photos by Stan Tekiela except pp. 56, 62 and 73 from Shutterstock

10 9 8 7

Bird Trivia: Funny, Strange and Incredible Facts about North American Birds
Copyright © 2018 by Stan Tekiela
Published by Adventure Publications
An imprint of AdventureKEEN
310 Garfield Street South
Cambridge, Minnesota 55008
(800) 678-7006
www.adventurepublications.net
All rights reserved
Printed in China
ISBN 978-1-59193-810-1 (hardcover); ISBN 978-1-59193-811-8 (ebook)

TABLE OF CONTENTS

Lazuli Bunting

THE MAGNIFICENT WORLD OF BIRDS

Birds are amazing creatures that have captured the hearts and minds of people everywhere. From their outrageous shapes and colors to their unique behaviors, birds are endlessly interesting! As a naturalist with more than 30 years in the field studying birds, I still continue to learn new and fascinating things about them.

What's not to like about a creature that is often brightly colored and sings beautiful songs? And what is more incredible than a bird's ability to fly? Birds are the only animals on the planet that have a lightweight coat of feathers. To be light enough for flight, they also have hollow bones and lightweight beaks. In this book, you'll discover many hundreds of other strange and wonderful tidbits about birds that you've always been curious to know.

In North America, we have more than 1,100 great species of birds to appreciate. Many hold astonishing North American records, and some also hold world records! Our winged friends are downright extraordinary, and now you can enjoy them even more with this fun collection of bird facts and light-hearted trivia.

Northern Cardinal

Bird Trivia
FUNNY BIRD BEHAVIORS

And the Oscar Goes To . . . The Killdeer! This eye-catching bird steals the show with its performance of a broken wing display. To draw an intruder or predator away from the nest site, Killdeer parents will fake an injury and flail about, dragging a wing on the ground. When their display leads the threat far enough away from the eggs or young, the parents suddenly become flightworthy and take off. Surprisingly, other birds, such as Snowy Owls, Mourning Doves and plovers, also feign broken wings.

Killdeer

Fights Its Own Reflection Some male birds, such as male Northern Cardinals, are known to fight their own reflections in a window, vehicle mirror or chrome hubcap. It is believed that these males see the reflection as a competing bird and attack it in an attempt to drive it off. Often this aggressive behavior continues for a couple of days, but sometimes it goes on for months at a time!

Anting for Hygiene Some birds perform a highly specialized behavior that may benefit feather health, called anting. After deliberately disturbing an ant mound, the birds will lie down and allow the ants to crawl all over them! Some of these birds crush the ants with their beaks and wipe the bug juices onto their feathers. It is thought that the formic acid discharged in the ants' defense acts like an insecticide, helping to eliminate ectoparasites in the feathers. Some believe it also acts like a fungicide or bactericide.

Where's the Sunscreen? Oddly enough, some birds lie down in the sun and just stay there for a couple of minutes. They choose a sunny spot, spread their wings and tails, open their mouths, and usually close their eyes. This behavior is known as sunning. Many theories attempt to explain why birds do this, but most likely it just feels good.

Ruby-throated Hummingbird

Bathroom Break Time Vultures have a strange and unusual behavior of urinating and defecating on their legs and feet. The action is actually a means of cooling down by way of evaporative cooling. Called urohidrosis, the birds do this during hot weather, when they are overheating. The Wood Stork also does this to keep cool.

Hawking for Food Flycatchers and other birds that mainly eat bugs will hunt flying insects in a technique called hawking. These birds simply perch on a branch and wait for an insect to pass by. When a bug comes near, they quickly dart out to snap it out of the air, and then return to the branch to eat.

Funny thing, Red-headed Woodpeckers do the same exact thing even though they're not flycatchers, and they don't have a main diet of insects.

Birds Using Tools Some gulls will carry clams or oysters high above the ground and drop them onto rocks to break open the shells. Crows use twigs to fish insects out of cracks and crevices.

Fearless Snake Hunter The roadrunner uses a bizarre method to hunt venomous snakes. It will fluff its feathers, spread its wings and taunt the snake to strike! The bird tries to keep far enough away so that when the snake strikes, it may only graze the feathers, missing the skin. A roadrunner will make a

Greater Roadrunner

snake strike three or four times to wear it down or continue to taunt until the striking stops. At that point, the roadrunner uses its large bill as a weapon and strikes the snake's head a couple of times. Afterward, it picks up the snake and whips it around until it is dead.

Killer Songbirds   Most predatory birds have strong feet and long, sharp talons to grasp and dispatch prey. Shrikes are predatory songbirds that lack this equipment, but they still capture and kill smaller birds and rodents successfully. Loggerhead and Northern Shrikes, also called Butcher Birds, have long, heavy bills with a sharp hook on the end to do the job. Once they subdue the prey, they usually impale the meal on a stout thorn or barbed wire, where they tear it into small, bite-sized pieces.

Northern Shrike

Preening: More Than Just Cosmetic   All birds preen their feathers with their bills and feet to keep them in good condition. Some species, such as Great Blue Herons, Barn Owls and American Bitterns, also have a specialized middle claw with a serrated edge that serves as a built-in comb. These birds use the comb-like edge as a preening tool on their heads to rid themselves of debris or parasites. This special claw is called a pectinate claw, or feather comb.

One Leg to Stand On   Nearly all birds will, at times, draw one leg up into their belly feathers for warmth and remain standing on the other leg. Large birds, like hawks and eagles, will slip a leg into their feathers to keep it warm, but it's the shorebirds that are known for this. After tucking a leg, they often bury their bills into their back feathers and take a little nap. Some shorebirds keep one leg tucked even after being disturbed and hop away on the other leg.

Red Knot

9

Foot Waggling Some species, such as the Common Loon, almost always have their feet in water. These birds do a funny-looking behavior known as foot waggling. Sometimes they will lift a foot out of the water and shake off the excess water droplets. Then, they

Common Loon

wag it back and forth many times, making it look like they're waving with their foot! Afterward, they tuck the foot under their wing feathers to keep it warm.

Courtship Dancing Chicken-like birds, such as Greater Prairie-Chickens, Sharp-tailed Grouse and Sage Grouse, perform some of the more elaborate courtship displays in the bird world. Males gather in an open area, called a lek, to dance and strut, and sometimes, to fight for the admiring females. The word "lek" comes from the Swedish *leka*, which means "to play." The same leks are often used over and over again by many generations of dancing males.

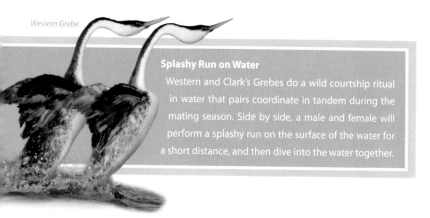

Western Grebe

Splashy Run on Water

Western and Clark's Grebes do a wild courtship ritual in water that pairs coordinate in tandem during the mating season. Side by side, a male and female will perform a splashy run on the surface of the water for a short distance, and then dive into the water together.

Mixing Up Some Eggs Some birds not only lay eggs in their own nests, but they also lay some in the nests of other females in their species. Hooded Mergansers, Wood Ducks and Common Goldeneyes will even lay some of their eggs in the nests of other species! This behavior, known as egg dumping, can result in Wood Ducks incubating Hooded Merganser eggs, Hooded Mergansers incubating Common Merganser eggs, and any number of mixed-up combinations.

Sounds Like Spring Thunder In spring, the male Ruffed Grouse will stake out a fallen log deep in the forest to perform a mating display. Unlike woodpeckers, which drum on objects with their bills to communicate, the grouse quickly flaps its wings to make drumlike sounds. But the sounds aren't made by the wings flapping against the chest (like Tarzan beating on his chest), because they never touch the chest. The grouse flaps forward so fast that it forces a pocket of air between its chest and wings. This is the action that creates the sound waves we hear as low, drumming thuds. Knowing this, it's no wonder that the Ruffed Grouse is also called the Spring Thunder.

Ruffed Grouse

Bird Trivia
WILD ADAPTATIONS

Osprey "Fingerprints" The Osprey is a fish-eating raptor with special feet. Small, spine-tipped projections, called papillae, on the bottom of their feet help them hold their slippery fish prey. The patterns of papillae are unique to each individual bird. So just as fingerprints identify people, Ospreys can be identified by their papillae prints!

Shock Absorbers Needed Experiments on Red-headed Woodpeckers show that they have the highest g-forces (g's) of all woodpeckers. When pecking wood, they hit trees with an impact velocity of up to 20 times per second about 12,000 times a day! This subjects the brain to a deceleration of around 1,000 g's. By comparison, astronauts on space shuttles experience 3.5 g's during takeoff.

Woodpeckers have a spongy pad between the bill and the skull that helps absorb shock. They also have lightweight brains without a lot of mass, so their brains don't hit the inside of the skull very hard with each blow. In addition, they have an extremely long tongue that wraps around the outside of the skull and anchors at the base of the bill. This provides even more shock-absorbing properties.

Head-Turners No, owls cannot twist their heads all the way around, as some people think. With 14 vertebrae in their necks (people have half as many), owls can turn their heads to an incredible 280 degrees!

Snowy Owl

Climbing Shoes Bird claws are well adapted for daily activities. Birds that climb tree trunks, for example, have claws that are more curved compared with those of non-climbing species. Nuthatches, creepers, and even some warbler species, such as the Black-and-white Warbler, are tree climbers, and they all have modified claws.

White-breasted Nuthatch

One Big, Long Claw!
Nuthatches have an extra-long, curved hind claw, or nail, on their feet. This specialized claw not only allows the birds to climb headfirst down a trunk to look for food, but also to hang upside down on suet feeders and such.

Weight Trimmers Birds have several modified body parts that reduce their weight and make flying more efficient. First and foremost, they have hollow bones (pneumatic bones). To give strength and rigidity to the bones, there are struts, or branches, on the inside.

In addition, birds have a strong, yet lightweight, beak. The beak tears and slices through food, functioning in much the same way as teeth. Birds also use their beaks to carry materials for nest building, as well as food to the babies in the nest.

Birds are covered with a coat of feathers. Feathers are an efficient, lightweight body covering. Hollow bones, lightweight beaks and feathers help reduce the overall weight of birds, which, at the same time, gives them the freedom of flight.

Not all birds, however, have hollow bones. Some aquatic birds, such as loons and penguins, have semisolid bones (semipneumatic bones), making them heavier than other birds of similar size. The added weight increases their density, which makes their bodies ride lower in water and decreases the amount of energy needed to swim underwater, where they spend much of their life.

Shivering The thermoregulation system of birds is very different from that of mammals. In mammals, the digestion of food in the gastrointestinal tract produces heat and keeps the internal temperature at around 98 °F. Birds, however, shake and shiver the muscles in their bodies to maintain a much more cozy body core temperature of about 106 °F.

House Finch

Some Fat Is Good! Birds have large deposits of white fat in their bodies, mostly concentrated in the chest. White fat fuels flight and provides birds with the energy they need to shiver their muscles to keep warm.

NOT FUSSY ABOUT FISH

Freshwater and Saltwater Fare Most birds are diet specialists that stay near a food source to feed on specific foods. Some other birds, namely Common Loons, live in freshwater from spring until fall, where they feed on freshwater fish. In late fall, they move to the ocean and spend the winter feeding on saltwater fish. It is highly unusual to switch between freshwater and saltwater diets! Loons have specialized glands near their eyes that excrete the excess salt ingested from the seawater habitat.

Black-capped Chickadee

Torpor Shutdown Some birds, such as Black-capped Chickadees, go into a state of torpor at night during extremely cold weather. During the evening, the birds enter a sheltered cavity or similar place to spend the long night. Sometimes they huddle with other birds to share body heat. The birds will shiver to keep warm, but they interrupt it with periods of inactivity, causing the body core temperature to drop slightly. As they alternate shivering with staying still, the heart rate and respirations decrease along with their reducing temperature. When they reach a full state of torpor, they lose consciousness.

The more their body temperature drops, the more precious fat they save, which they use for energy. Toward morning, the birds start shivering again. As this increases, the body core temperature rises. When the birds are fully out of torpor, they leave the shelter and go about their day.

Webbed Swimmers Loons have large, fully webbed feet. When a Common Loon pushes off to swim, each foot opens like a parachute to capture the maximum amount of water. When the foot is drawn back, it collapses to a fraction of the inflated size, reducing drag and helping the loon cruise through the water.

Walking (Almost) on Water Purple Gallinules are wonderfully colored birds of the swamps in the Deep South. They have very long toes, over 4 inches in length, which help distribute their weight. Their long toes give them the uncommon ability to walk on floating lily pads without sinking.

Purple Gallinule

Elf Owl

Bird Trivia
RECORD HOLDERS

The Shortest-Lived Bird The most short-lived birds are the humming-birds. On average, Ruby-throated Hummingbirds live only three to five years.

The Smallest Owl The Elf Owl of southwestern states and Mexico is the smallest owl in North America and the world. About the size of a sparrow, it's just 5 inches tall and weighs only 1 to 1½ ounces, or 28 to 43 grams.

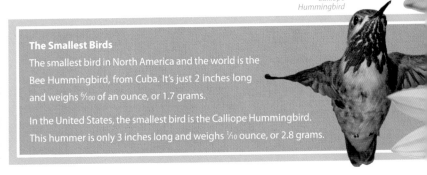

Calliope Hummingbird

The Smallest Birds

The smallest bird in North America and the world is the Bee Hummingbird, from Cuba. It's just 2 inches long and weighs ⁶⁄₁₀₀ of an ounce, or 1.7 grams.

In the United States, the smallest bird is the Calliope Hummingbird. This hummer is only 3 inches long and weighs ¹⁄₁₀ ounce, or 2.8 grams.

The Rarest and the Longest-Lived In North America, there are fewer than 300 California Condors in the wild. This makes the condor our most uncommon bird. Condors live about 60 years in the wild. They live longer in captivity, with some reaching 80 years of age or more!

California Condor

The Most Abundant Bird Red-winged Blackbirds may have the highest number of individuals in the United States. The overall population has been estimated to be more than 100 million birds! In addition, it is estimated that some wintering roosts have more than 1 million birds. Some researchers believe that the Common Grackle might be just as numerous.

Red-winged Blackbird

The Most Common Shorebird The Killdeer is the most common and widespread shorebird, but it doesn't live at the shore. It's seen at farms, railroad tracks, empty lots with gravel and other dry places.

Barn Owl

The Best Mouser
It may be impossible to know which owl species eats the most mice. One study, however, estimated that a Barn Owl could eat more than 11,000 mice over a 10-year span!

The Strongest Food Grinder Since birds don't have teeth, they can't chew food before they swallow it. Instead, they have a sort of pre-stomach, called a gizzard, which grinds their food into smaller particles. The strongest gizzard on record belongs to the Wild Turkey. It can crush whole acorns still in the shell in fewer than four hours!

The Most Successful Mover The Eurasian Collared-Dove has been very successful at expanding its range all by itself, without introduction to new places by people. Originally a native of northern India, it spread into southern Europe by the sixteenth century. It took a long time, but by the 1930s it became widespread across most of Europe, reaching Britain by the 1950s. It began breeding in Iceland in the 1970s and was inadvertently introduced to the Bahamas at that time. By the 1980s, it was breeding in Florida. Since the 2000s, it has moved into many other parts of the United States.

Eurasian Collared-Dove

The Most Exotic Birds

Peach-faced Lovebird

With nearly 70 kinds of exotic birds, the United States has the most non-native or introduced species in North America. These include the House Sparrow, European Starling and Peach-faced Lovebird.

Brown Pelican

Bird Trivia
RARE AND EXCEPTIONAL BIRDS

Headfirst Diver The Brown Pelican is a diving feeder and the only pelican that dives headfirst into water to catch fish. In the 1970s, it faced extinction due to DDT poisoning. Today, laws protect this bird, and it's doing much better.

In contrast to the Brown Pelican, the American White Pelican is a dipping feeder that swims and dips its head into the water to catch fish.

America's Only Avian Hibernator The only known hibernating bird in the United States is the Common Poorwill. A member of the nightjar family, the poorwill lives in the deserts of the Southwest. At the beginning of winter, it chooses a spot on a rocky, south-facing cliff or hides under a large shrub. Just like a hibernating mammal, its heart rate drops, respirations decrease and its body core temperature falls. In this bird, hibernation lasts upwards of four months.

North America's Only Aquatic Songbird
The American Dipper is the only truly aquatic songbird. It dives under the rushing water of mountain streams to catch aquatic insects to eat. It does this all year, even in winter! It also sings a lovely song from the banks of the streams.

American Dipper

Canada Jay

Bird Trivia
WAIT, WHAT'S THAT BIRD CALLED?

Hell-diver The Pied-billed Grebe is a waterbird that's also known as the Hell-diver. Long ago, when hunters shot at these birds, they ducked beneath the surface so quickly and remained underwater for so long that the hunters thought they dove down to hell!

Pied-billed Grebe

Formidable Monikers The Greater and Lesser Roadrunners are the only species of roadrunners in North America. Expert hunters, they are also called the Snake Killer, Chaparral Cock and Ground Cuckoo.

Camp Robbers Clark's Nutcrackers and Canada Jays share another name: Camp Robber. Both birds are friendly and will approach camps to find food, grab it and fly away. They are even known to land on an outstretched hand offering peanuts.

Pigeon? Or Dove? Technically, there isn't any difference. Pigeons and doves are closely related. The term "pigeon" is reserved for the larger, dove-like birds.

Cobs and Pens Male and female swans have peculiar names. The males are called cobs. Females are pens.

Chick Colts Crane chicks, called colts, are the only birds that share the same name as young horses.

Sandhill Crane

Song Sparrow

Bird Trivia
BIRDSONG, CALLS AND MORE

The Most Prolific Songster Birds are well known for their amazing songs. The Brown Thrasher is the most prolific songster and an expert mimic, with an impressive repertoire of more than 1,100 songs! The thrasher is so good at vocal mimicry that some people can identify the species that actually sings it. A thrasher will repeat each phrase of a song twice before singing the next phrase.

Learning from the Best Many young songbirds will learn their tunes by listening to the adults, but not necessarily their parents. Song Sparrows learn their eight to ten songs from the dominant males singing in the area, which may not include their male parent.

Brown Thrasher

Who's That Singing? The Northern Mockingbird is another remarkable mimic. This bird hears other species singing in the vicinity and learns to sing their songs. A very wonderful man once told me that if you have a mockingbird around your house, you don't need any other songbirds. The mockingbird repeats phrases up to six times before moving on to the next one.

Northern Mockingbird

Singers Are Usually Male Both male and female Northern Cardinals sing beautiful songs. Purple Finches, Gray Catbirds, Baltimore Orioles and Rose-breasted Grosbeaks are other species in which the male and female sing. This is strange, but most female songbirds in North America usually don't sing. Oddly enough, in other parts of the world, such as Europe and Asia, the females sing just as much as the males! This makes our female songbirds unusual.

Northern Cardinal

Duet Singing In a few select species, mated pairs will sing back and forth to each other. This behavior is called duet singing. Northern Cardinals are famous for it, and Carolina Wrens do it regularly. The male wren starts out with a three- or four-note song that repeats several times. His female partner joins in at just the right time with a buzzy, high-pitched trill, which lasts well into the second phrase of the male. Together they defend their territory with their duets.

Mute Birds

While many birds are known for their wonderful songs, others are silent more often than not. Vultures, such as Turkey Vultures, are mostly mute, making only occasional grunts and groans.

Turkey Vulture

Singing with a Mouthful Birds have a specialized voice box, called a syrinx, located at the far end of the trachea near the lungs. The syrinx divides into two chambers. In each chamber, sounds are produced independent of each other. Birdsong is fully developed in the syrinx before it reaches the beak. This makes it possible for many birds to grip food with their beaks and still sing a full song at the same time.

Yellow Warbler

Wing Singing The male American Woodcock, also known as the Timber-doodle, performs a sky dance for females in spring and serenades them without using his voice. He has several modified primary flight feathers that are unusually narrow and stiff. In his aerial courtship display, the male rapidly flutters his wings. When air vibrates over the feathers, it produces a twittering noise, like a unique mating song.

Two-Part Melodies Many birds, such as Wood Thrushes, sing a song that's actually two separate songs. The most incredible part about this is that they sing both songs at the same time! Each half of the vocal box produces one song, and they both blend together to make up the full song.

Wood Thrush

Counter-Singing Matches Marsh Wrens, a tiny brown bird of cattail marshes, learns the songs of other males and sings them nearly identically.

29

Marsh Wren

With more than 100 melodies in their songbooks, the males often sing identical tunes back and forth to each other to impress the females with their musical abilities. This behavior of sending and receiving songs is called counter-singing.

Same Song, Only Different We often hear birds of the same species singing the same song. Male Indigo Buntings, for example, are bright blue songbirds that are known for their marvelous song. The tune is composed of a few notes and phrases that repeat several times. When the songs of different males were examined as sonograms, however, they told a very different story. Each male had actually been singing his own individual song, with varying phrases, notes, length and content.

Indigo Bunting

The Loudest Voice Most people would agree that the Sandhill Crane has the loudest call of all birds, but they may not know why. The Sandhill has a trachea longer than that of any other bird, and it acts like a trumpet. When a Sandhill Crane calls from the ground on a calm morning, it can be heard up to 2½ miles away! While flying, the call can be heard even farther out.

Sandhill Crane

Drumming Out a Notice Woodpeckers drum on hollow logs, branches, stovepipes and other resonating objects to send out loud messages. A woodpecker drumming gives clear notice to other woodpeckers of the same species about its territory and its availability to mate.

Hairy
Woodpecker

American Woodcock

Bird Trivia
AMAZING ANATOMY

Golden Eagle

The Best Eyesight It is generally thought that birds of prey, such as eagles, hawks and falcons, have the best sight of all birds. The Golden Eagle can spot the movement of a rabbit over 1½ miles away. The Peregrine Falcon can see a pigeon flying in the sky more than 5 miles away!

Visual acuity is measured by the number of light-sensitive rods and cones in the back of the eyes. Raptors have many more of these structures than we do, allowing them to resolve details two to three times better than we can from far distances. People have about 200,000 light-sensitive receptors per square millimeter, while small birds, such as sparrows, have around 400,000. Birds of prey, such as eagles, have the greatest visual acuity, with over 1 million receptors per square millimeter.

Twice-as-Good Focus One area in the back of our eyes, called the fovea, is packed with cone cells and increases our visual acuity. The fovea allows us to look at something closely and see it clearly, such as reading the text on this page. Most birds, however, have two foveae in the back of their eyes. This increases their ability to see things up close and farther away more sharply.

Winner of 360-Degree Vision The American Woodcock has the greatest field of vision not only in North America, but also in the entire bird world. It has large, bulbous eyes, which allow it to see a full 360 degrees, as well as straight up overhead. This means it can see in all directions without moving its head!

What's to See in UV Light? Three types of color receptors enable people and birds to see red, green and blue. However, a fourth type of receptor in birds allows them to detect ultraviolet (UV) light, which is something that we can't see. It is thought that nearly all birds have the ability to see in the UV spectrum of light.

Blue Jay

Seeing in UV light has several advantages for birds. Many flowers reflect UV light, revealing dark lines that point directly to the nectar within. Hummingbirds, as well as insects, use their UV vision to find their nectar meals. Fresh urine reflects bright yellow in UV light. Raptors that hunt small mammals, such as mice and voles, easily see these deposits and follow them to the prey.

UV light also penetrates heavy cloud cover. This helps migrating birds determine the position of the sun and allows them to continue on their migration route on cloudy days.

In many species, the males and females appear exactly the same to people. Scientists think that these seemingly identical birds, such as male and female Blue Jays and American Crows, see color differences in plumage with the aid of UV light, helping them to differentiate the sexes.

Built-in Sunglasses

Birds have a unique oil droplet in the cone receptors in their eyes, providing a shield against UV light. For birds, this is like having built-in polarized sunglasses!

Osprey

Best Color Vision The ability to see colors depends on receptors in the eyes, called cones. Animals with more cones have better color vision. Humans have three types of cones, while many other mammals have just two types. Birds have four types of cones, giving them some of the best color vision on earth.

Harris's Hawk

Telephoto-Like Shape In some birds of prey, the eyes are tubular rather than round, like human eyeballs. Like a telephoto lens of a camera, the distance from the lens at the front to the retina at the back is increased in tubular eyes, enhancing bird vision.

Outrageous Proportion Birds have extremely large eyes in proportion to their heads, especially raptors. If we had the same proportion as raptors, our eyes would be more than eight times larger, making each one about the size of an orange! The size of a bird's eyes indicates the utmost importance that vision plays in its world.

Best Vision in the Dark In low-light conditions, nocturnal birds have the best vision. No bird can see in complete darkness, but owls have the best light-gathering ability and visual acuity. They have more light-sensitive cells packed onto their retinas than we do. In controlled experiments, some owl species were able to see prey in only 1 percent of light.

Eyes in Back of the Head The American Kestrel is a small falcon that has two small dark spots on the back of its head, called ocelli. Because it is said that these spots resemble eyes, they're often called false eyes. False eyes make the kestrel appear like it is looking back when it's actually looking ahead.

American Kestrel

Ferruginous Hawk

Extra Set of Eyelids In addition to a set of regular eyelids, nearly all birds have an extra eyelid on each eye, called a nictitating membrane. This whitish, or sometimes clear, membrane closely conforms over the eyeball and can be drawn over the eye to help clean, moisten and protect it. Most birds blink their membranes so quickly that it's not noticeable to the human eye. Other birds, such as owls and hawks, blink them slow enough to see. Some birds, such as ducks and loons, close their membranes over their eyes when diving for protection underwater.

Some Eyes Change Colors Many hawks, such as Sharp-shinned and Cooper's Hawks, have yellow eyes in their first two to three years of life, and red eyes as adults. The males often turn red before the females, but some slower-maturing individuals can take as long as five years to change. In some species, such as the Bald Eagle, young birds start out with brown eyes. These eventually turn yellow, taking five years or more to change. The eyes of Red-tailed and Swainson's Hawk juveniles change from pale yellow to dark brown at adulthood.

The Best Sense of Smell Most birds have a poor or reduced sense of smell. The region in the brain for processing odors is extremely small, and birds have very little nasal surface area to boot. Some birds, however, namely vultures, have a well-developed sense of smell. Soaring high up, a Turkey Vulture can smell rotting flesh at more than 5,000 feet in the air—almost a mile above the ground! Interestingly, when a natural gas pipeline springs a leak and spews foul-smelling gas, Turkey Vultures are fooled into thinking there is something dead and rotting to eat.

Safety Filters for Nostrils All birds have nostrils, called nares, at the base of their bills. The shape and size of the nasal openings are different in each species. In many birds, such as woodpeckers, tufts of feathers cover the nares and conceal them. When woodpeckers excavate cavities and the wood dust is flying, the feathers act like a protective filter.

Shut-Off Valves for Divers Some diving birds, such as loons, have a small flap that covers each nare and shuts out water during a dive. Each flap, called an operculum, needs to be strong enough to withstand the pressure of swimming underwater.

Acorn Woodpecker

Tough Enough to Protect Some birds, such as hawks, have a leathery band of skin, called a cere, at the base of the bill and surrounding the nares. Because the cere is tough, it is thought to help protect the nares. The cere is often brightly colored.

Sharp-shinned Hawk

Who "Hears" What? Smaller birds are usually more sensitive to high-frequency sounds, while larger birds tend to sense low frequencies better. It is believed that they may be detecting these sounds via a receptor in their bodies rather than actually hearing the sounds with their ears.

It is thought that birds can sense low-frequency sounds produced by distant storms, alerting them of adverse weather to come. Some species respond to severe weather warnings by moving hundreds of miles away to safety. After the storm has passed, they return.

The Best Hearing It is very likely that the night-hunting owls, such as Barn, Long-eared and Boreal Owls, have the best hearing in the bird world. Many of these nocturnal owls have asymmetrical ear openings, with one opening higher and one larger. These allow sound to enter their ears at very slightly different times, helping them to accurately triangulate the position of their prey.

In laboratory tests, a Barn Owl was able to catch live prey in total darkness just by using its hearing. It could pinpoint the sound of prey moving on both vertical and horizontal planes to within one degree of accuracy. When sound entered its uneven ears at minutely different times, the owl could hear the delay in one ear in as little as 100 microseconds!

Boreal Owl

Stop That Noise Pollution! If you are an owl, sensitive hearing is good for hunting in the dark, but what do you do when you want to sleep during the day? All owls have small, skin-like flaps, called opercula, to cover their ear openings. These allow the birds to shut out sound and take a break from the cacophony of their world.

The Bill, aka Beak The bill, also called a beak, is unique to the bird world. Some reptiles, such as turtles, have a similar mouthpart, but only the bills of birds have a wide variety of shapes and colors. The bill is composed of an upper and lower beak. The upper bill usually overlaps the lower when the mouth is closed. A bird's bill continually grows and is worn down by daily activities, such as feeding, foraging and grooming. If a bill doesn't get worn down, it will grow too large to be useful.

What? The Bill Has a Covering? Bills are joined to a boney core that is attached to the skull. The bill has a covering, called the rhamphotheca, which is more like a sheath and grows throughout the life of a bird. The rhamphotheca is usually hard and hornlike and includes the tip and biting edges of the bill. However, in some birds, such as the ducks, sandpipers and pigeons, it is softer and more leathery.

Seasonal Bill Colors Like plumage, the bill covering of some species changes colors with the seasons. Atlantic, Horned and Tufted Puffins have some of the most colorful bills during the breeding season, and much duller bills afterward. American Robins and European Starlings have bright yellow breeding bills that turn gray for the winter. Evening Grosbeaks have lime-green bills that turn bright yellow after the breeding season, and breeding House Sparrows and Bobolinks have black bills that later become yellowish. The sheath of the duller, non-breeding bill wears away in spring, and a new, brighter sheath grows over it for the breeding season.

His and Hers Bills
Male and female Mallards have different colored bills. During the breeding season, the male's bill color ranges from olive-green to yellow. The female has a bright orange bill with black spots.

Mallard

In the Mouths of Babes In most species, begging nestlings have bright red, orange or yellow oral flanges. Looking like lips, the colors serve as a target area for the parents to feed. In other species, nestlings have a bold red lining in their mouths. During mealtime, the color attracts the eyes of the parents and helps the nestlings get more food.

Birds Don't Have Lips Some people mistakenly think that hummingbirds use their bills like a straw to suck nectar. This is physically impossible, however, because like other birds, hummingbirds don't have lips. Instead, hummingbirds dart their tongues in and out of nectar at an unbelievably fast rate of 10 times per second! Hummingbirds have tongues with narrow channels along the sides, and with each quick dip into nectar, the channels fill. Each time the hummers draw their tongues back into their mouths, the nectar is stripped out and swallowed.

Serrated Bills Common Mergansers have long, narrow bills with serrated edges. They use the serrations like teeth to hold slippery fish.

Crossed Bills Red and White-winged Crossbills are northern finches with odd-looking crossed bills. When their mouths are closed, the tip of their upper bill crosses down over the lower bill, and the tip of the lower bill crosses up over the upper.

Red Crossbill

In other species, a crossed bill would be considered a deformity. In crossbills, the arrangement works great for extracting pinecone seeds, their main food, from the cones. To get the seeds, crossbills push their bills under the scales of closed pinecones and bite to separate the scales. When the seeds are exposed, they use their tongues to extract them.

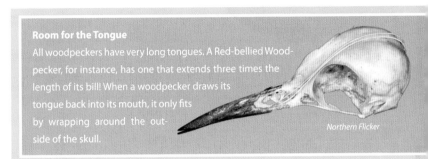

Room for the Tongue
All woodpeckers have very long tongues. A Red-bellied Woodpecker, for instance, has one that extends three times the length of its bill! When a woodpecker draws its tongue back into its mouth, it only fits by wrapping around the outside of the skull.

Northern Flicker

The Strongest Bill Woodpeckers have larger and stronger bills than other birds. Not only do they use their bills to excavate holes in trees for nesting, but they also drum on resonant objects with their bills to communicate with other woodpeckers.

The Biggest Bill The American White Pelican has an enormous orange bill. The lower bill has a pouch of skin, called a throat sac, which fills with water when the pelican fishes for food. When the bird closes its bill, the water is pushed out of the sac and gushes out over the sides of the bill.

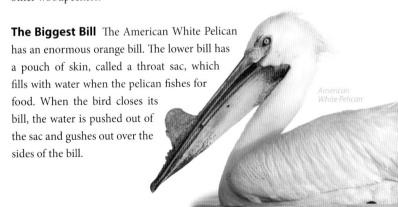

American White Pelican

During the breeding season, a knob, or horn, grows on the upper bill. After breeding, the knob falls off. This American White Pelican is the only pelican that grows a breeding knob.

Long Bills in Shorebirds

Most people know that shorebirds have long bills, but not many know that the Long-billed Curlew has one of the longest. It has a very long, down-curved bill that measures 5 to 8½ inches. The bill looks a bit unwieldy because the head is tiny in comparison. The curlew uses its bill to reach insects buried in mud or underwater.

Long-billed Curlew

Caution: Up-Curve Ahead Like many waterbirds, the American Avocet has a long, thin bill. But this bird is one of the few with a curved bill that goes up rather than down. The avocet swishes its bill back and forth in shallow water, stirring up aquatic insects to eat before snapping its bill down on the prey.

Perfect for Skimming One of the most unique bills belongs to the Black Skimmer. The skimmer is a very distinctive-looking shorebird with a long and extremely thin bill. Unlike other birds, which have a longer upper bill than lower, the skimmer's lower bill is longer than the upper. The skimmer will fly low over the water with its mouth open, skimming water with its lower bill. The narrow shape of the bill allows the bird to slice through the water with little drag. When it feels a fish, it snaps the bill shut to catch a meal.

Black Skimmer

Beak like a Parrot The Atlantic Puffin has such a funny-looking red and black beak, some people affectionately call it the Clown of the Sea or the Sea Parrot. The upper beak has special serrations that help the bird carry as many as 10 slippery fish to its young in the nest.

Built-in Spoon The Roseate Spoonbill, a large, pinkish wading bird, has one of the most unique bills of all birds. Shaped like a large spoon, the bill functions like a filter and a trap. To locate food, the spoonbill swings the tip of its bill back and forth in shallow water. When it senses a small fish or an aquatic insect, it snaps the bill shut quickly, flushing out the water while retaining the morsel.

Roseate Spoonbill

The Shortest Legs The Chimney Swift has some of the shortest legs of all of our North American birds, measuring less than half an inch! It has very short legs and strong feet, which allow it to cling tightly to vertical surfaces, such as chimneys.

The Longest Legs In North America, the Black-necked Stilt has the longest legs relative to the body length. The legs of this bird make up about 60 percent of its height! Whooping Cranes, Sandhill Cranes and Great Blue Herons are other species in North America that have some of the longest legs.

Black-necked Stilt

Aquatic Bird Feet Most aquatic birds, such as ducks, have webbed feet. The webbing is a thin, membranous skin that attaches at the toes and stretches out in between. In ducks, geese and gulls, three of their four toes are webbed. In pelicans and cormorants, all four toes are webbed. Webbing helps aquatic birds swim faster by providing more surface area for water contact, giving each foot a canoe-paddle effect.

Aquatic Bird Legs The legs of some aquatic birds, such as most ducks, are located directly beneath their bodies and hang straight down, allowing for efficient movement when paddling. This also helps them walk well on land.

The legs of other aquatic birds, most notably loons and grebes, are set far back on the body and well off to the sides. This design enables strong paddling strokes with no interference from the opposite returning webbed foot. These birds hold their wings against their bodies when underwater, reducing drag, while their powerful legs and large feet propel them to catch even tiny darting fish. On land, however, the birds are slow and clumsy.

Boots and Leggings Bird legs and feet are unique, but not all species have the same kind of protective covering, or podotheca. Some have tough, leathery skin. Others have scales, like reptiles. Still others have papillae, which are spiny protuberances. Usually these coverings are mainly on the feet.

Robins thrushes have a smooth and continuous covering, like boots, called a booted covering. Ospreys have a network of small, irregular patches, called reticula. Most other birds have overlapping scales, called scutella. No matter the type, each covering is durable and very resistant to abrasion.

American Robin

Insulated Feet and Legs In some birds, such as ptarmigans and owls, extra feathers cover their legs, and especially their feet and toes. These provide added insulation and offer more surface area for support, like snowshoes, when the birds walk on snow.

Great Horned Owl

Cold Water Circulation How can ducks and geese swim in near-freezing water without losing all of their body heat, and not freeze their feet? In countercurrent circulation, warm arterial blood from the heart passes right next to cold blood returning from the toes, transferring heat.

Weak Feet Even though vultures are included in the raptor group, they don't share some important characteristics with the other birds of prey. Hawks, eagles, owls and the other raptors have strong feet and long, sharp talons for capturing and dispatching prey. Vultures, on the other hand, have weak feet and short talons, making them incapable of killing with their feet.

Walking on Toes We humans are plantigrade, walking on the soles of our feet. Birds, however, are digitigrade. They walk on their toes. Birds have four (or three) toes on each foot. Only a few species, such as the Three-toed Woodpecker, have three toes.

Classic Toes The normal position of the four toes is three pointing forward and one pointing back, called anisodactyl. Most small songbirds and some hunting birds, such as eagles, hawks and falcons, have this arrangement.

Climber Toes Parrots, woodpeckers, roadrunners and other birds that climb a lot have a zygodactyl toe arrangement, which is two toes pointing forward and two pointing back.

Varied Thrush

45

Reversible Toes Owls have an anisodactyl arrangement—most of the time. Sometimes they swing their outermost front toe around to face back, changing to the zygodactyl position. Owls use this position to grip a perch, as well as to capture prey.

Fused Toes The toes of the Belted Kingfisher are arranged in the typical anisodactyl form, but toes two and three are fused together for part of the toe length. Partially fused toes help this cavity nester to dig out a long tunnel leading to an earthen nesting chamber.

Belted Kingfisher

Superlong Toes Chimney Swifts have unusual feet with four superlong toes that all point forward. Called pamprodactyl feet, the toe arrangement allows swifts to cling to vertical surfaces, usually the inside of chimneys or hollow tree trunks. They can also move their toes independently, maneuvering toes one and two against toes three and four to form a pincer-like grip. This ability helps them carry and manipulate nesting material.

Ruffed Grouse

Scaly Toes
Ruffed Grouse have scales on their toes that enlarge during winter. Like snowshoes, toe scales provide more surface area and help support the weight of the grouse on snow.

Lobed Toes Grebes and coots have lobed toes, not webbed feet, like ducks. The lobes are loose flaps of extra skin around each toe that remain separate from the adjacent toes. Lobed toes provide more surface area for the birds to push against water and propel themselves forward.

Chimney Swift

Nail Hooks

Talons don't always need to be long and strong for killing. The talons of Chimney Swifts, more appropriately called nails, are long and curved and act like hooks. Swifts use their hook-like claws to hang in hollow niches, like chimneys, where they get some sleep for the night.

That Duck Has Claws? The Wood Duck has classic webbing on its feet just like other ducks, but it also has extra-long claws! This bird is a tree nester that spends a lot of time during the breeding season high up in trees. It uses its claws to climb around the branches as easily as it walks on the ground.

Some Big Claws! Bald Eagles have extremely long, very sharp talons for holding prey tightly and dispatching it. Each of their toes has a fierce-looking talon that's over 2 inches long. Eagles sink their talons deep into their prey, piercing the vital internal organs for a quick kill.

Bald Eagle

47

Light as a Feather Everyone knows that feathers are lightweight. But did you know that an entire coat of feathers accounts for just 5 to 10 percent of a bird's weight? This means that a Black-capped Chickadee with a weight of $\frac{4}{10}$ ounce, or 11 grams, would have a feather coat weighing $\frac{2}{100}$ to $\frac{4}{100}$ ounce, or .5 to 1 gram. The weird thing is, a bird's ridiculously lightweight coat of feathers is still two to three times heavier than its entire skeleton!

Ruby-throated Hummingbird

The Least Feathers As you might have suspected, the smaller the bird, the fewer the feathers—and vice versa. The record holder for the fewest feathers goes to the hummingbirds. The Ruby-throated Hummingbird, for instance, has about 1,000 total feathers. In contrast, the Trumpeter Swan, which is the largest waterfowl in North America, has more than 25,000 feathers.

Leucistic Coloration
A leucistic bird has aberrant feather coloration, typically white to off-white or color-faded to washed out. Leucism can affect just a few feathers or nearly all feathers. A leucistic bird only has partial pigment loss and is not the same as an albino, which has all types of pigment loss, including in the eyes.

Sandhill Crane

More or Less Feathered In most bird species, the number of feathers varies with the season. Birds have more feathers in winter, which helps keep them warm. In addition to the extra winter feathers, aquatic birds, such as ducks and geese, have more feathers than similar-sized terrestrial birds in spring, summer and fall. All of these extra feathers help them stay warm in cold water, no matter the time of year.

Fluffy Down Down feathers are the small feathers closest to the body of a bird. Down lacks the tiny interlocking barbs (barbules) that are present in flight feathers. Soft, fluffy down has some of the best insulating properties of all known materials and provides the insulation that helps keep birds warm.

Not Your Usual Feathers Bristle feathers are a very different kind of feather, and not all birds have them. Usually on the head or face, they are small, stiff feathers that look like whiskers or hairs. It is assumed that these feathers act similarly to the whiskers of mammals. Most night-flying birds, such as owls and nighthawks, have bristle feathers.

Short-eared Owl

The Stiffest Feathers Woodpeckers have the stiffest feathers of all the birds. Their feathers are always in contact with wood, so they need to be tough. Premature wear and loss of feathers would disable these birds and eventually would be fatal.

Woodpecker feathers are so inflexible that they create a noisy flight. When a woodpecker flies to your feeder, you may hear it before you see it. If you find a woodpecker feather on the ground, you can even feel the rigidity.

Skin Heads A few bird species lack feathers on their heads. Vultures are the prime examples. They feast on carrion and often poke their naked heads into gashes of dead bodies. Scientists have long thought that the naked head of vultures reduces the risk of feather fouling from contact with blood and other body fluids. But why is it that Wild Turkeys have featherless heads? They feed on insects, seeds and fruit—not carcasses.

Recent research has proposed that a bird's naked head may also help regulate body heat. Vultures draw their heads down into their neck feathers to keep warm on cold nights, and they raise their heads high to stay cool on hot days. In the same way, it's likely that the naked heads of Wild Turkeys may also help regulate their internal thermostat.

Black Vulture

Wild Turkey

Wood Duck eclipse

Eclipse Plumage Most male ducks, such as male Northern Pintails and Wood Ducks, molt their fancy feathers in late summer and look similar to the duller females. This is called eclipse plumage. The drab, non-breeding plumage of these males is said to eclipse their eye-catching breeding plumage. But don't worry. By midwinter, the males will be back to their full breeding plumage again.

Wood Duck breeding

Northern Hawk Owl

Bird Trivia
FEATS OF FLIGHT

The Fastest Flier Clocked at over 180 mph in diving flights, the Peregrine Falcon is the fastest bird in North America and also the world. It flies high up to hunt for other birds, and then dives to extreme speeds toward its prey. This hunting dive is called a stoop. With balled feet, it strikes the prey, knocking it out of flight and sending it crashing to the ground. Sometimes it might even snatch the prey right out of the sky.

Peregrine Falcon

Silent Hunting in Flight Owls are known for their silent flight. These nighttime hunters have a modified, serrated leading edge of their primary flight feathers that helps break up wind turbulence created during flight. This, combined with a fuzzy trailing edge of feathers and a soft, velvety cushion between the feathers, creates silent flight.

Takeoff from the Water Several species of aquatic birds, such as the American White Pelican and Common Loon, will run on the surface of the water to take off. These birds face into the wind and start to run while they flap. It usually takes a few seconds before they sail up and away. Without wind, it takes more running and more time to take off.

Common Loon

The Heaviest Bird in the Sky When it comes to the heaviest flier in North America, it's a close call between two species. The California Condor weighs 28 to 31 pounds, making it the winner. The Trumpeter Swan is the runner up, weighing 24 to 28 pounds.

Trumpeter Swan

Both birds are excellent fliers, but the condor has the advantage of extremely long wings. Stretching out over 9 feet, this wingspan is wider than that of all other North American birds. So a prize for the greatest wingspan goes to the California Condor as well.

California Condor

Swift in the Air Chimney Swifts spend most of their lives flying. They hunt for insects, drink, perform courtship displays and even copulate in flight. During the breeding season, they are often seen flying in small groups of five or six birds, called a squadron. Later, after the young have left the nest, the families fly together. When hunting for prey, however, swifts often do it on their own.

The Most Time Flying In North America, the Magnificent Frigatebird will fly for more than two months without landing! Also called the Pirate of the Sky, it stretches out its wings to a 7½-foot span and soars over the ocean in search of fish. This bird manages to eat, bathe and even sleep while it flies.

Magnificent Frigatebird

The Fastest Birds in a Beeline There is little agreement about which bird is the fastest flier in level flight. Golden Eagles are said to fly upwards of 90 mph, but so do Gyrfalcons. Magnificent Frigatebirds can reach over 90 mph at times, and Rock Pigeons are reported to clock in at about the same speed. Even Red-breasted and Common Mergansers can be super speedsters, flying in straight lines at more than 80 mph.

How Birds Hover Many species of birds, such as the American Kestrel, can hover for short periods of time with the help of the wind. These birds will fly into a headwind and remain stationary relative to the ground. This is called wind hovering. Larger birds, such as Golden Eagles, Red-tailed Hawks and Gyrfalcons, can also do this with enough of a headwind.

Golden Eagle

Hummingbirds are the only birds that can truly hover in place without a headwind. Under controlled conditions, one hummingbird hovered continuously for 50 minutes!

The Fastest Flapper
You guessed it! Hummingbirds have the fastest wingbeats. They flap their wings at a mind-blowing 80 times per second during normal flight, and more than 200 times per second during courtship flight.

European Starling

The Most Acrobatic By far, hummingbirds are the most versatile in flight. They are the only birds that can fly straight up, straight down and backward. They also hover without a headwind, and they can even do aerial somersaults! Unlike other birds, hummers move their wings in a figure-eight pattern instead of flapping up and down. This utilizes both the upstroke and downstroke to produce thrust and gives them the ability to do fantastic acrobatics.

Clouds of Birds Some birds, such as blackbirds and starlings, fly in large flocks of often thousands of individual birds, called a murmuration. A murmuration looks like a dazzling, swirling cloud as the birds fly around in the sky. How the birds don't run into each other is still a mystery!

European Starling

Kettles in Thermals Some larger birds that migrate during the day, such as American White Pelicans and Broad-winged Hawks, travel in flocks. They search out rising columns of warm air, called thermals, and ride to the top, often a thousand or more feet high. They swirl around and around in a thermal, getting higher and higher until they reach the cooler air at the top. There, the birds fly off to ride another thermal.

A flock of birds in a thermal is called a kettle. Some say the movement of the birds swirling to the top and flying off is reminiscent of water boiling to the top of a kettle and spraying out.

Snow Goose

Bird Trivia
MIGRATION
HALL OF FAME

Is It Time to Migrate Yet? Many people mistakenly believe that changing weather or food shortages trigger migratory behavior. But weather and food supplies are not consistent from year to year. Besides, shorebirds migrate south in mid to late summer, when the weather is still warm and food is still plentiful. So how do birds know when it's time to migrate? For most birds, the trigger is the amount of daylight from sunrise to sunset, called the photoperiod. Changes in the photoperiod are consistent from year to year, making it a reliable natural indicator.

Restless to Migrate When the photoperiod indicates that the time to migrate is drawing near, the migratory birds become restless. During this phase, called migratory restlessness, the birds feed heavily, building up fat for the trip, and orient themselves on branches or perches and when roosting at night, facing in the direction they will be heading.

Built-in Magnetic Compass You have to wonder how birds find their way to places they've never been to before. Migration is still not fully understood, but research has shown that birds have some kind of built-in magnetic compass to help guide them along their way. Pigeons, however, have small, magnetically sensitive areas in the tip of their bills and in the front of their brains. With these, they sense the Earth's magnetic field. This helps them navigate and keeps them going in the right direction.

Rock Pigeon

Natural Road Signs By itself, a built-in compass isn't enough for successful navigation during migration. Birds use the stars to help them at night, but most likely there is much more to the entire process. Some migrators may also be listening for moving rivers or crashing oceans to help keep them on course.

All Speeds Are Legal There are about as many migratory flight speeds as there are species of birds. In general, the smaller the bird, the slower the flight will be. During spring, migration is like a race to return to the breeding grounds. The fall migration has a more laid-back approach. Either way, some smaller birds migrate about 60 to 80 miles in a day. Larger birds, such as hawks, cover upwards of 250 miles daily.

Flight at Night Most of our small songbirds migrate in the darkness of night. The cooler nighttime temperatures help prevent overheating during flight, and the steadier winds help push the birds along. During the day, night migrators search for food and get some rest.

Red-tailed Hawk

MIGRATOR MYTH DEBUNKED

Don't Believe It! Ruby-throated Hummingbirds do not migrate on the backs of Canada Geese. This long-held notion is just not true. Ruby-throats leave at the end of summer and migrate all the way to Central and South America. Most Canada Geese migrate only a couple hundred miles and leave well into fall, long after the hummingbirds are gone.

Migratory Flyways Most birds follow migratory flyways. There are four major corridors that facilitate the movement of large numbers of birds. The **Atlantic Flyway** extends from the eastern United States and Canada down through the Caribbean into many parts of South America. In central parts of the United States and Canada, the **Mississippi Flyway** follows the Mississippi River and crosses the Gulf of Mexico, reaching into South America. The **Central Flyway**, sometimes called the Missouri Flyway, stretches from the Missouri River to the Rockies, extending up into Canada and down through Mexico into Central America. The **Pacific Flyway** runs along the West Coast from Alaska and Canada into western South America.

Migration Formations Larger daytime-fliers migrate in formations. Some species, such as the American White Pelican and Snow Goose, fly in large V shapes. The Snow Goose migrates in huge V formations or sometimes in just one angled line. Flying in formations allows the birds that are following other birds to save energy during flight.

Most of our small birds don't fly in formations. They fly alone or with other birds that just happen to be flying in the same direction at the same time.

Snow Goose

The Largest Migratory Flocks During migration, Snow Geese travel in the largest flocks. Flocks of more than 100,000 Snow Geese are common in the spring migration northward. In some areas, such as Nebraska, flocks with millions of geese have been reported.

Arctic Tern

Stopovers along the Way Natural migratory rest stops are crucial places where migrators can stop, eat and rest. Unfortunately, with the constant development of housing and shopping areas, these areas are becoming fewer and farther between. Birds are forced to travel farther without a break before finding a good place to stop.

Yellow-bellied Sapsucker

The Longest-Distance Woodpecker
The Yellow-bellied Sapsucker migrates farther than any other woodpecker. It flies from the northern tier states and Canada to as far south as Central America.

The Longest-Distance Migrator The winner for the longest migration goes to the Arctic Tern. This bird nests in the far North, well into the Arctic Circle. Most of these birds fly over the Atlantic Ocean to the Antarctic and back, racking up around 50,000 to 60,000 miles. This is twice the circumference of the planet! Others that nest in Alaska fly down the Pacific Coast to the Antarctic and back in a similar record-breaking distance. Over an average lifetime of 30 years, the Arctic Tern will fly more than 1.5 million miles. This is more than three times the distance from Earth to the moon and back.

The Longest Distance Nonstop The Bar-tailed Godwit makes the longest nonstop migration. In the fall, starting from its breeding grounds in Alaska, it flies more than 7,000 miles over the Pacific Ocean all the way to New Zealand without stopping for food, water or rest! This arduous journey usually takes about two weeks. During spring, the godwit takes a different route home that offers rest stops.

Marsh Wren

Bird Trivia
ALL ABOUT NESTS

The Tiniest Nest It makes sense that the tiniest birds, which are hummingbirds, make the tiniest nests. The nest of a Ruby-throated Hummingbird is around the size of half of a walnut shell—only 1½ inches wide! A female Ruby-throat lays two eggs and builds the nest to fit her body. Since the babies will stay in the nest until they reach adult size, she uses plenty of spider silk. This lets the nest stretch and expand along with her growing young.

Ruby-throated Hummingbird

The Largest Nest Bald Eagles make the largest nests of all birds. They use their nests for many years, even decades. The largest Bald Eagle nest ever recorded was constructed near St. Petersburg, Florida. In 1963, it measured more than 9 feet wide and 20 feet deep, and was estimated to weigh nearly 3 tons!

So Many Choices! The tiny male Marsh Wren builds around 25 ball-shaped nests with a side entrance for prospective females to evaluate. He constructs them in stands of cattails in wetlands, occasionally refurbishing old nests. The female chooses one, and then lays her eggs. The other nests, called dummy nests, are left as is to confuse predators.

Enter through the Tunnel The Belted Kingfisher digs a narrow tunnel in a riverbank or dirt cliff that ends in a nesting chamber. Some of these tunnels extend more than 10 feet, but on average, most are 3 to 5 feet long.

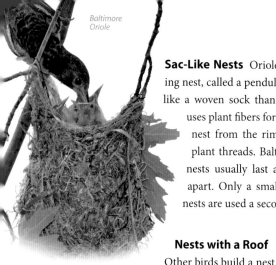
Baltimore Oriole

Sac-Like Nests Orioles weave an intricate hanging nest, called a pendulous nest, which looks more like a woven sock than anything else. The female uses plant fibers for materials and suspends the nest from the rim with meticulously woven plant threads. Baltimore and Orchard Oriole nests usually last about a year before falling apart. Only a small percentage of pendulous nests are used a second time.

Nests with a Roof

American Dipper

Other birds build a nest with a roof, called a domed nest. American Dippers, Ovenbirds and Eastern Meadowlarks do this. The American Dipper gathers moss and builds its nest near splashing water. Water keeps the moss soft, damp and alive, and prevents the nest dome from becoming dry and collapsing.

Must-Have Accent Materials Some birds, such as House Sparrows and European Starlings, gather bits of paper and plastic to add to their nests. Tree Swallows search for errant bird feathers to line their nests and will travel great distances to find them.

House Sparrow

THE BROOD PARASITE

It's Not a Nester The Brown-headed Cowbird is a brood parasite. Instead of building a nest and raising a family, the female seeks out the nests of other birds, lays an egg and leaves. A cowbird female can lay 40 or more eggs in just one season! Cowbirds are known to lay eggs in the nests of over 200 other species. Nearly 150 species will accept the eggs and raise the cowbird young.

Nest Recycling Most nests are temporary structures, built for one breeding season. Nests hold the eggs during incubation and provide a safe place for flightless baby birds. In most species, once the young leave the nest, they don't return to it.

Other nests are used repeatedly. Some species, such as the Red-tailed Hawk, use the same nest for many years, renovating it as needed.

Woodpeckers are primary cavity-nesting birds. This means they excavate their own nest cavities, and they are the primary users. Most woodpeckers use their cavities just once to incubate and raise the young. If they nest a second time in the same season or during the following spring, they excavate a second cavity. After they vacate the premises, other birds, such as House Wrens and Eastern Bluebirds, use the cavities.

House Wren

Pileated Woodpecker

Bald Eagle

The Oldest Nests A Bald Eagle nest in Vermilion, Ohio, was once used for 35 years in a row! Some Osprey nests have been used for more than 40 years, but not consecutively. Some Peregrine Falcon scrape nests have been used for nearly 50 years.

Waste Management Many species of birds try to keep their nests clean. This can be challenging when young birds have nowhere to eliminate their waste. The babies of some species, such as the White-breasted Nuthatch and Common Grackle, lift up their bottoms and produce a fecal sac, which the parents promptly grab and carry away. A baby bird's digestive system is not operating at peak performance yet, so many nutrients are expelled in the packets. Some adult birds will consume the sacs and gain the benefits from the extra nutrients.

Northern Flicker

Indigo Bunting

⚞ Bird Trivia ⚟
BABIES ON THE WAY!

An Egg a Day All birds, including our domestic chickens, lay only one egg per day. Some species take two (or even three) days between egg laying.

The Fewest Eggs The California Condor holds the record for laying the fewest eggs. The female lays just one egg per nesting season and usually nests only every other year.

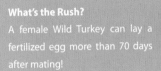

What's the Rush?
A female Wild Turkey can lay a fertilized egg more than 70 days after mating!

Wild Turkey

The Shortest Incubation Some small birds, such as buntings, finches and wrens, incubate for about 11 days before they hatch. This is the shortest incubation period.

Interestingly, J. J. Audubon reported that a Ruby-throated Hummingbird incubated for 11 days, making it the shortest incubation on record. He also reported that the male Ruby-throat fed the female and the chicks. He got these wrong because we know now that Ruby-throats take 12 to 14 days to incubate, and male hummers don't take any part in incubating or raising their young.

Northern Bobwhite

Wandering Albatross

The Longest Incubation Generally, the larger the egg, the longer it takes to hatch. The California Condor incubates close to 60 days. The Wandering Albatross, a large seafaring bird found in Hawaii, takes upwards of 80 days.

Synchronous Hatching Some birds, such as robins, bluebirds and cardinals, don't start sitting on their eggs until all of the eggs have been laid. These birds can take more than a week to lay their eggs. Once all of the eggs are laid, the female will start incubating the clutch at the same time. This results in all of the babies hatching at the same time. This is called synchronous hatching.

Asynchronous Hatching Some of the larger birds, such as eagles and owls, nest earlier in the year when temperatures are still cold. To keep their eggs from freezing, these birds start incubating immediately. The first egg laid will hatch before the last one laid hatches. The amount of time between the first egg hatching and the last one to hatch matches the time intervals when the eggs were laid. This is called asynchronous hatching. It produces some young that are more than a week older than the other siblings in the nest.

Time to Break Out! An egg tooth is a very small, sharp projection on the upper part of a baby bird's upper bill. A bird about to hatch will slowly turn around in the eggshell, with the egg tooth inscribing a circle around one end. With a push and a shove, the baby breaks through at the perforation. After the bird hatches, the egg tooth is no longer needed and falls off shortly afterward.

Northern Bobwhite

Common Loon

Bird Trivia
REARING THE CHICKS

These Hatchlings Need Help Baby birds that hatch with a minimum of feathers and their eyes sealed shut are called altricial young. These helpless birds need their parents to keep them warm, fed and safe. Altricial chicks often need to stay in the nest for several weeks or more before they are able to leave for their first flight.

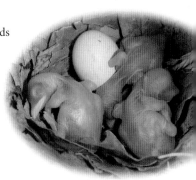

Purple Martin

Precocious Baby Birds Many birds, such as ducks, geese, cranes and loons, produce hatchlings that are covered in feathers and can walk or swim right after hatching. These babies are called precocial young. After hatching, precocial birds usually stay in the nest for just 24 hours before they head out into the world. They often feed themselves and get around their environment just as well as their parents.

Jump, Little Ducklings! Some duck species, such as the Wood Duck and Common Goldeneye, nest in tree cavities. Their nests are often higher than 30 feet above the ground! Soon after hatching, the ducklings leap from the rim of their nest down to the ground, where the mother waits to lead them to the nearest pond or lake. These babies are so tiny and lightweight that they don't get injured from their plummeting fall.

Wood Duck

Ruby-throated Hummingbird

Regurgitation Feeding Many species of herons and egrets will catch a fish and swallow it whole. After feeding, the parent returns to the nest to feed the young. The hungry youngsters pull violently on the parent's bill. This stimulates regurgitation of the entire fish.

Several smaller species, such as the American Goldfinch, regurgitate a half-digested seed mixture to their nestlings. Hummingbirds regurgitate a mixture of partially digested insects and sugar-rich nectar. A baby hummer opens its beak, and the mother slides her long bill down the baby's throat in what looks like a sword-swallowing act!

What? The Male Doesn't Help? In many species of birds, the males help raise the young. Woodpecker males incubate about 65 percent of the time, and they bring in more food than the females to feed to the chicks. In other species, the males have nothing to do with the incubating females or taking care of the young. This is true for all hummingbirds and most ducks.

Target Pecking Young Herring Gulls in the nest peck at the red spot near the tip of their parent's lower bill. Pecking the target stimulates the parent to regurgitate food for the babies.

Coming of Age The American Kestrel is a small falcon that starts to breed at one year of age. Other raptors, such as hawks, are usually three or four years old before they begin to breed. Eagles take a long time and are often over the age of five or six before they are sexually mature enough to mate.

Herring Gull

Bald Eagle juvenile

Sharp-tailed Grouse

ENJOYING THE BIRDS IN YOUR WORLD

North American birds have so many funny, strange and incredible attributes to marvel at and admire. This book has just peeled back the first of many layers of the amazing lives of birds and their crazy record-breaking records. Like me, you can spend a lifetime and still not explore all of the astounding feats and abilities of birds. However, learning about them makes for a fun and fulfilling journey.

I encourage you to get out and enjoy the birds that are around the area where you live. Better yet, set up a feeding station in your yard to attract birds so you can see them every day. While reading about birds is entertaining and enjoyable, nothing replaces the experience of observing birds and their behaviors firsthand. In all likelihood, you will see some of the species detailed in this book making their homes in and around your own backyard, while others are more far-flung across North America.

Enjoy the Birds!

ABOUT THE AUTHOR

Naturalist, wildlife photographer and writer Stan Tekiela is the author of the popular Wildlife Appreciation book series that includes *Bird Migration* and *Wild Birds*. He has authored more than 175 field guides, nature books, children's books, wildlife audio CDs, puzzles and playing cards, presenting many species of birds, mammals, reptiles, amphibians, trees, wildflowers and cacti in the United States.

With a Bachelor of Science degree in Natural History from the University of Minnesota and as an active professional naturalist for more than 30 years, Stan studies and photographs wildlife throughout the United States and Canada. He has received various national and regional awards for his books and photographs. Also a well-known columnist and radio personality, his syndicated column appears in more than 25 newspapers, and his wildlife programs are broadcast on a number of Midwest radio stations. Stan can be followed on Facebook and Twitter. He can be contacted via www.naturesmart.com.